What Bears

Written by Janelle Cherrington

SCHOLASTIC INC.

New York   Toronto   London   Auckland   Sydney
Mexico City   New Delhi   Hong Kong   Buenos Aires

PHOTO CREDITS: Front and back covers: © Daniel J. Cox/Natural Exposures; Title page: © Mike Macri/Masterfile; p. 2: © Gloria H. Chomica/Masterfile; p. 3: © Lisa Husar/DRK Photo; p. 4: © Johnny Johnson/DRK Photo; p. 5: © Dan Guravich/CORBIS; p. 6: © Daniel J. Cox/Natural Exposures; p. 7 © Michio Hoshino/Minden Pictures; p. 8: © Mike Macri/Masterfile.

ISBN 0-439-45517-0

1   2   3   4   5   6   7   8   9   10   08   11 10 09 08 07 06 05 04 03 02

Bears like flowers.

Bears like trees.

Bears like snow.

Bears like water.

Bears like berries.

Bears like fish.

Bears like bears.